The Very Best of
Creedence Clearwater Revival
EASY GUITAR WITH RIFFS AND SOLOS

Cover photo ©Photofest

ISBN 978-1-4234-4643-9

HAL•LEONARD®
CORPORATION

7777 W. BLUEMOUND RD. P.O. BOX 13819 MILWAUKEE, WI 53213

Visit Hal Leonard Online at
www.halleonard.com

Creedence Clearwater Revival

CONTENTS

Bad Moon Rising

Words and Music by John Fogerty

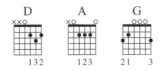

Strum Pattern: 4, 5
Pick Pattern: 1

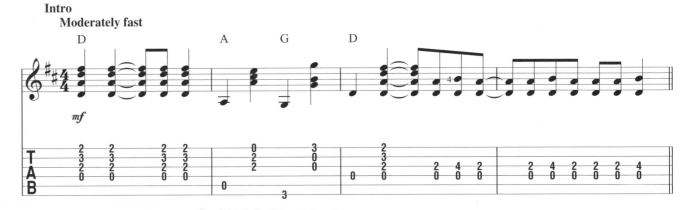

1. I see a bad moon a ris - in'. I see

2., 3. *See additional lyrics*

trou - ble on the way. I see earth - quakes and light -

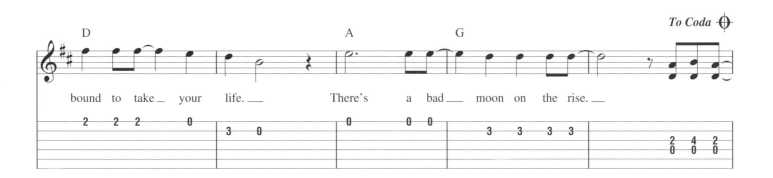

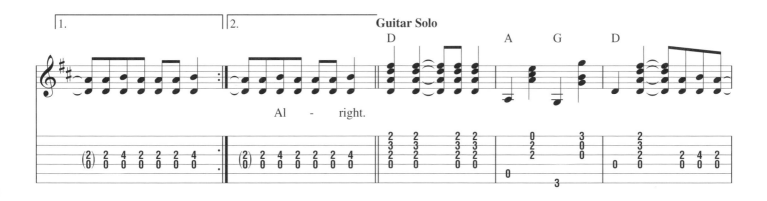

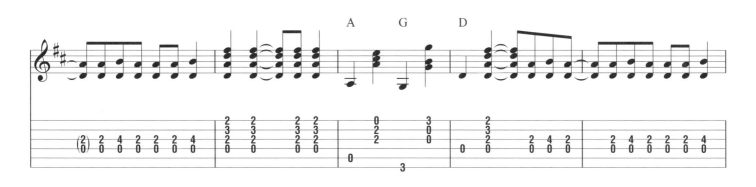

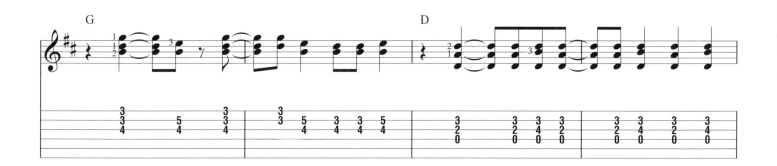

D.S. al Coda

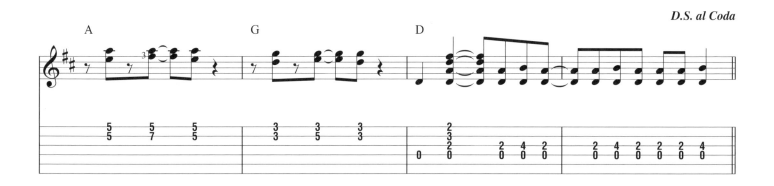

⊕ **Coda**

Outro-Chorus

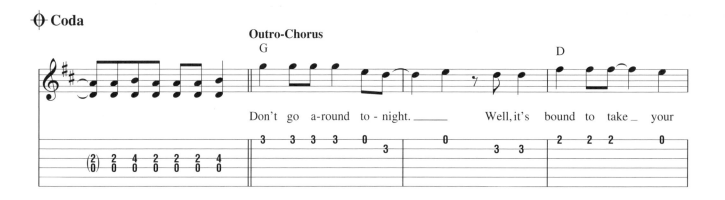

Don't go a-round to-night. _____ Well, it's bound to take _ your

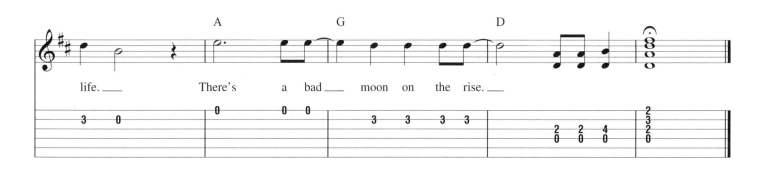

life. _____ There's a bad __ moon on the rise. _____

Additional Lyrics

2. I hear hurricanes a blowin'.
   I know the end is comin' soon.
   I fear rivers overflowin'.
   I hear the voice of rage and ruin.

3. Hope you got your things together.
   Hope you are quite prepared to die.
   Looks like we're in for nasty weather.
   One eye is taken for an eye.

Born on the Bayou

Words and Music by John Fogerty

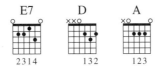

Strum Pattern: 3, 6
Pick Pattern: 3, 6

Intro
Moderately fast

let ring throughout Intro

1. Now,

Verse

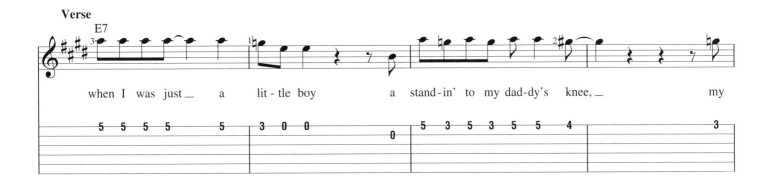

when I was just ___ a lit-tle boy a stand-in' to my dad-dy's knee, ___ my

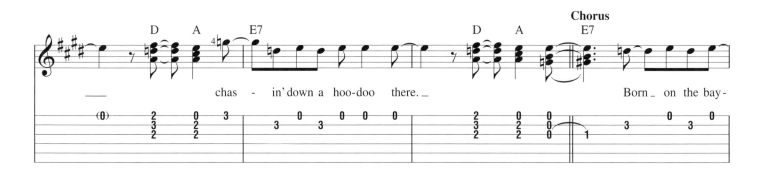

-ou, born on the bay-ou. Born on the bay-

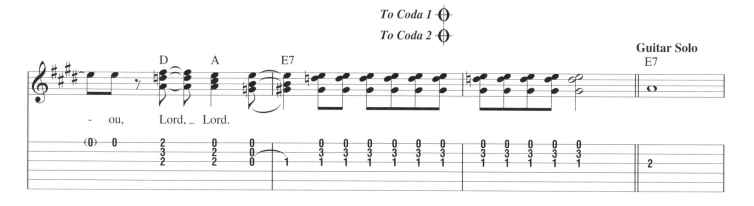

To Coda 1 ⊕
To Coda 2 ⊕

Guitar Solo

-ou, Lord, Lord.

let ring - - -

let ring

w/ pick & finger

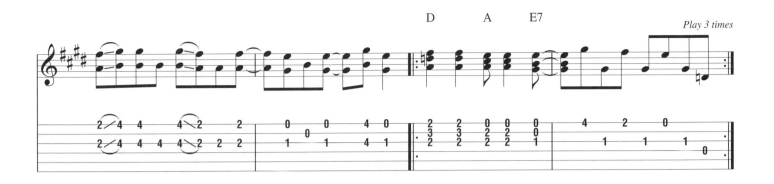

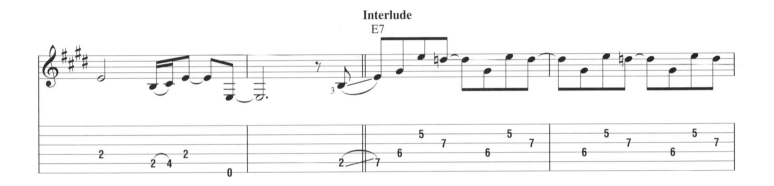

Coda 1

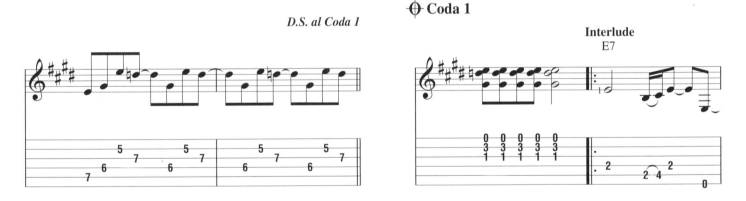

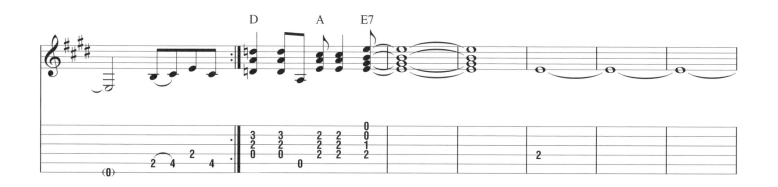

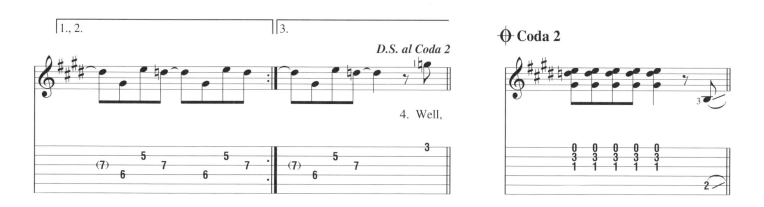

4. Well,

Additional Lyrics

3. Wish I was back on the bayou,
   Rollin' with some Cajun queen.
   Wishin' I were a fast freight train,
   Just a chooglin' on down to New Orleans.

Down on the Corner

Words and Music by John Fogerty

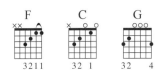

Strum Pattern: 6
Pick Pattern: 1

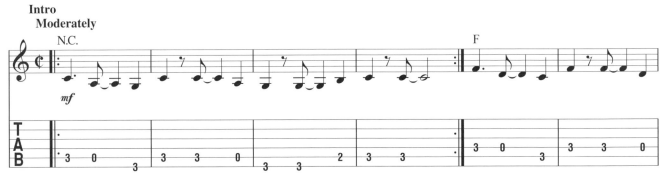

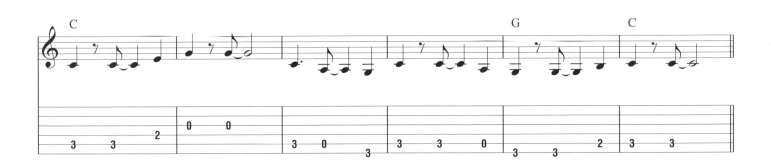

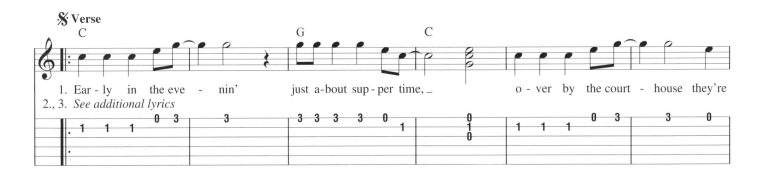

1. Ear - ly in the eve - nin' just a - bout sup - per time, __ o - ver by the court - house they're

2., 3. *See additional lyrics*

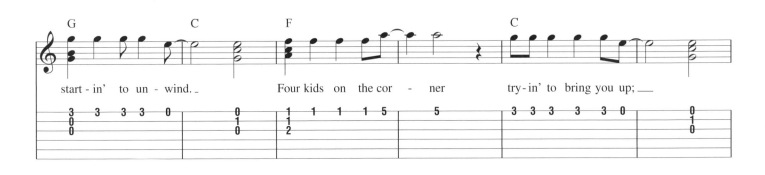

start - in' to un - wind. __ Four kids on the cor - ner try - in' to bring you up; __

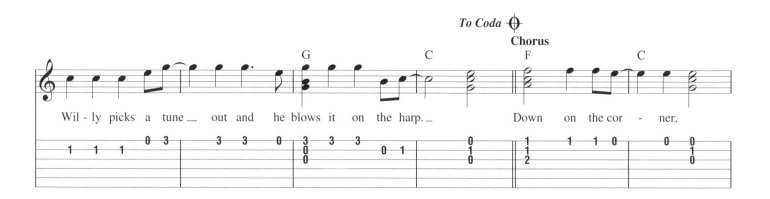

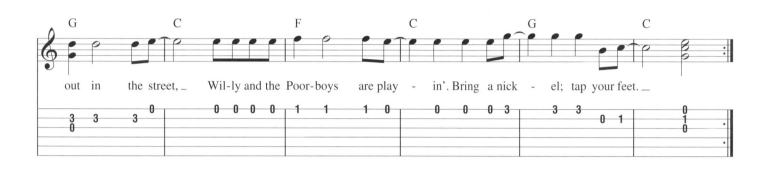

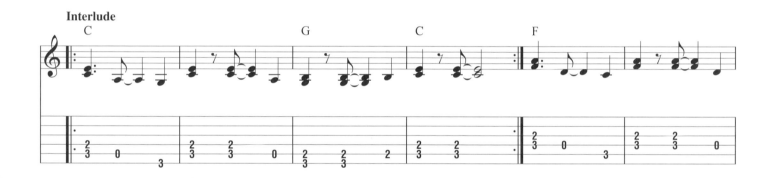

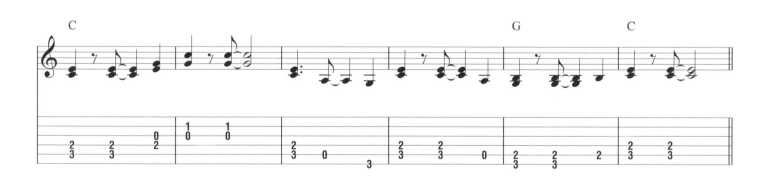

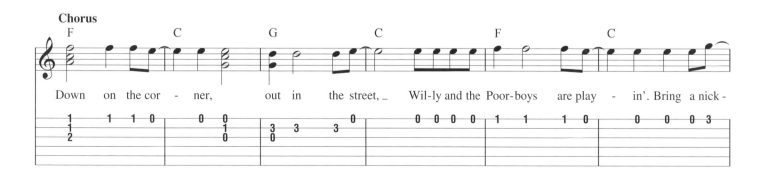

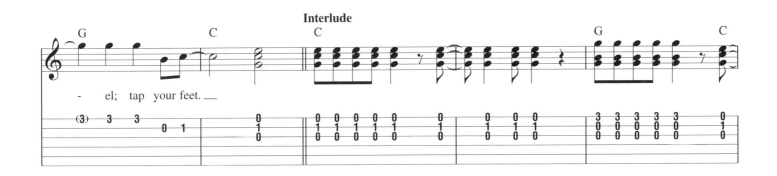

Interlude

-el; tap your feet. __

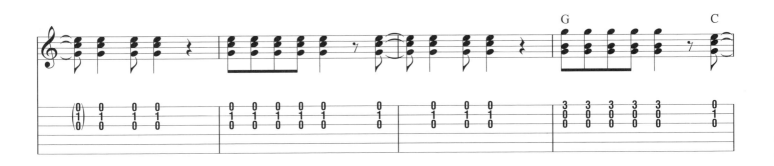

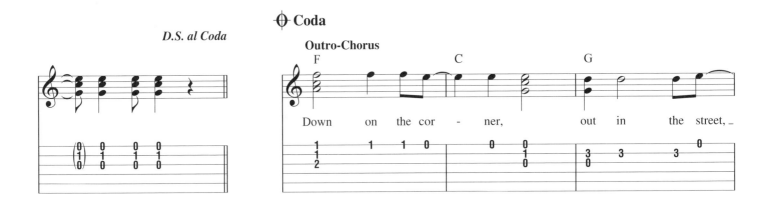

Coda

D.S. al Coda

Outro-Chorus

Down on the cor - ner, out in the street, __

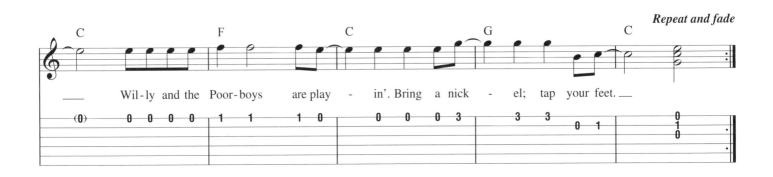

Repeat and fade

__ Wil-ly and the Poor-boys are play - in'. Bring a nick - el; tap your feet. __

Additional Lyrics

2. Rooster hits the washboard, people just gotta smile.
   Blinky thumps the gut bass and solos for a while.
   Poorboy twangs the rhythm out on his Kalamazoo.
   Willy goes into a dance and doubles on kazoo.

3. You don't need a penny just to hang around.
   But if you've got a nickel, won`t you lay your money down?
   Over on the corner there's a happy noise.
   People come from all around to watch the magic boy.

Green River

Words and Music by John Fogerty

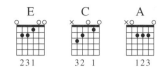

Strum Pattern: 1, 6
Pick Pattern: 6, 3

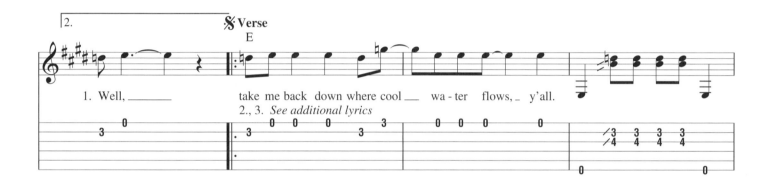

1. Well, _____ take me back down where cool ___ wa-ter flows, _ y'all.
2., 3. *See additional lyrics*

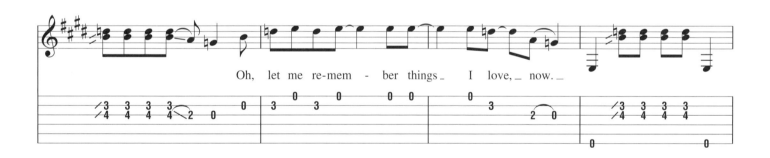

Oh, let me re-mem - ber things_ I love, _ now. _

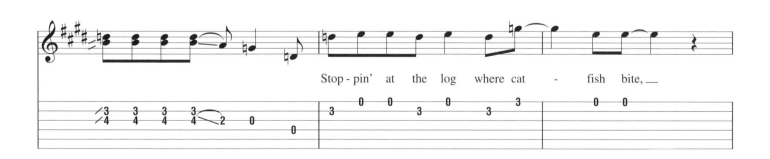

Stop-pin' at the log where cat - fish bite, __

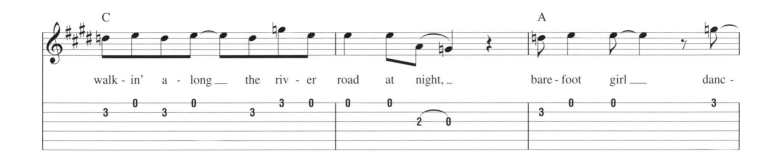

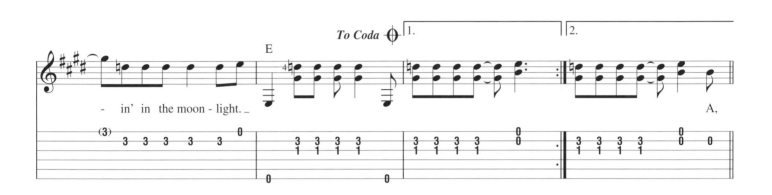

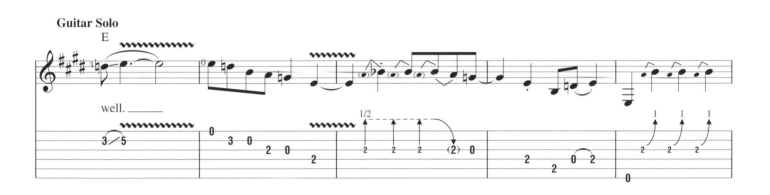

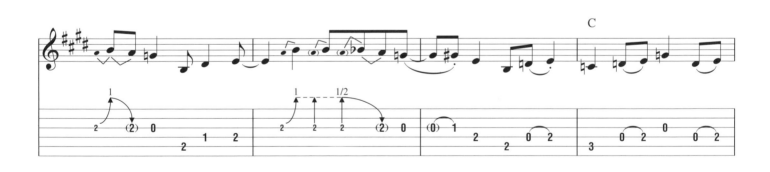

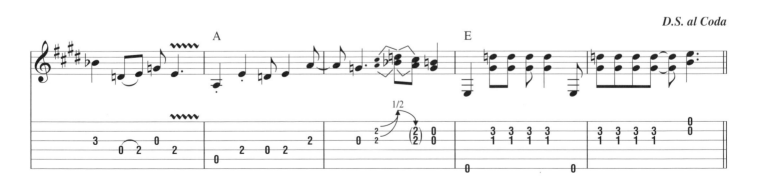

⊕ Coda

Outro-Guitar Solo

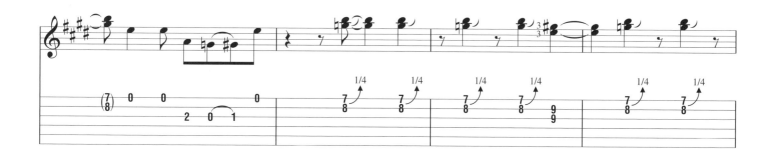

Additional Lyrics

2. I can hear the bullfrog calling me, how!
Wond'ring if the rope's still hangin' to the tree, oh.
Love to kick my feet way down the shallow water.
Shoo, fly, dragonfly, get back to your mother.
Pick up a flat rock, skip it across Green River.

3. Up at Cody's camp, I spent my days, oh,
With flatcar riders and crosstie walkers.
Old Cody Junior took me over;
Said, "You're gonna find the world is smould'ring,
And if you get lost, come on home to Green River."

Fortunate Son

Words and Music by John Fogerty

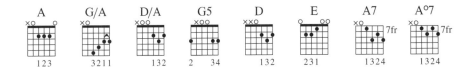

A   G/A   D/A   G5   D   E   A7   A°7

Strum Pattern: 4, 6
Pick Pattern: 4, 6

Intro
Moderately

(Bass & Drums)

f

let ring - - - - - - - - -

*Optional: To match recording, tune down 1 step.

𝄋 **Verse**

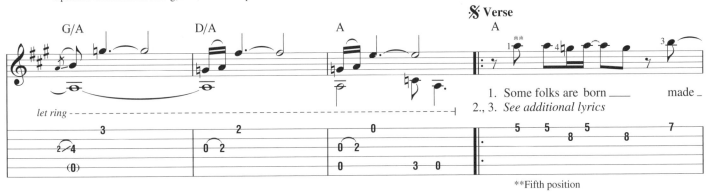

1. Some folks are born ____ made
2., 3. *See additional lyrics*

**Fifth position

let ring -

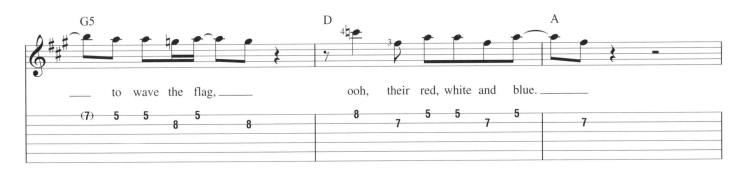

____ to wave the flag, _____ ooh, their red, white and blue. _____

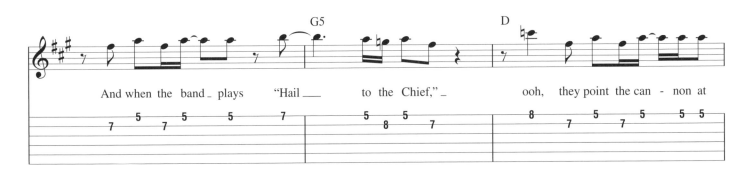

And when the band _ plays "Hail ____ to the Chief," _ ooh, they point the can - non at

Additional Lyrics

2. Some folks are born silver spoon in hand.
   Lord, don't they help themselves, y'all?
   And when the tax man comes to the door,
   Lord, the house looks like a rummage sale, yeah.

3. Yeah, some folks inherit star-spangled eyes.
   Oo, they send you down to war, y'all.
   And when you ask 'em, "How much should we give?"
   Oo, they only answer, "More, more, more, more."

Have You Ever Seen the Rain?

Words and Music by John Fogerty

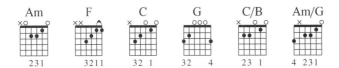

Strum Pattern: 1, 4
Pick Pattern: 2, 5

Intro
Moderately

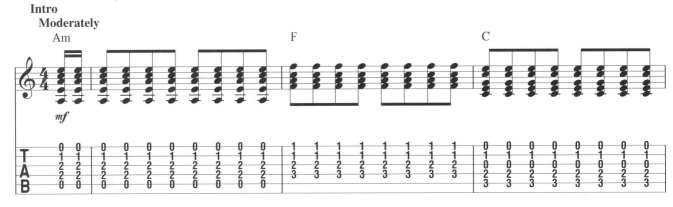

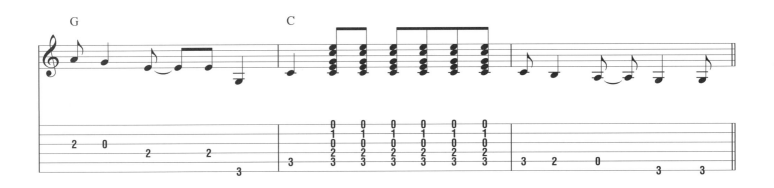

Verse

1. Some-one told me long ___ a - go, ___ there's a calm be - fore ___ the storm. ___ I know; ___
2. *See additional lyrics*

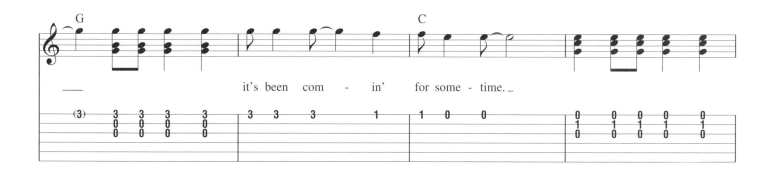

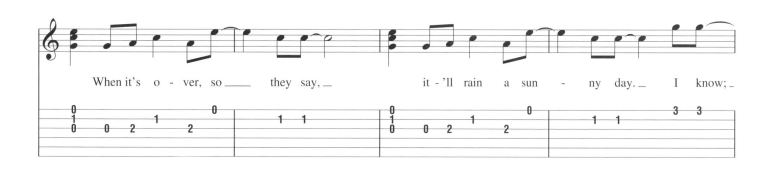

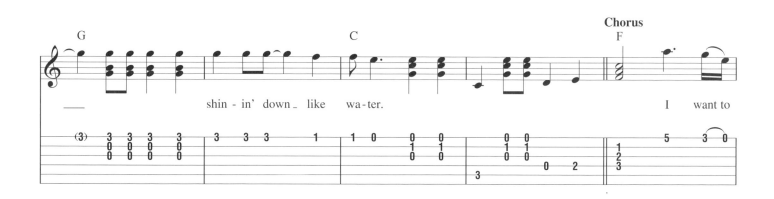

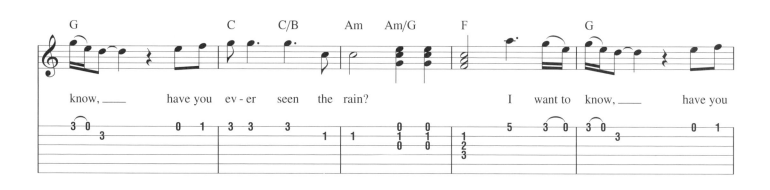

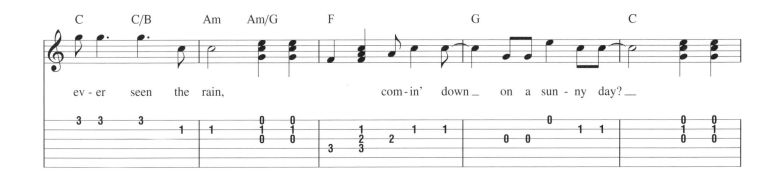

ev - er   seen   the   rain,   com - in'   down _   on   a   sun - ny   day? _

Outro-Chorus

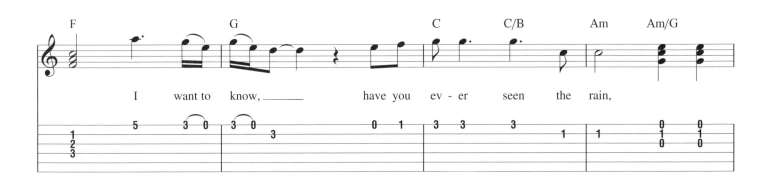

I   want to   know, ____   have you   ev - er   seen   the   rain?

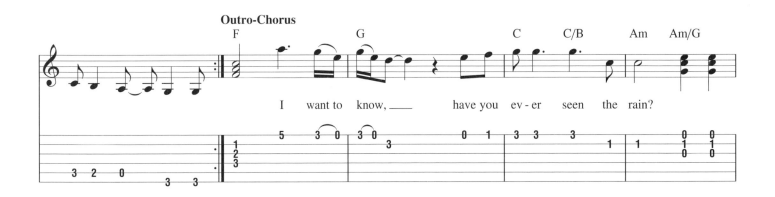

I   want to   know, _____   have you   ev - er   seen   the   rain,

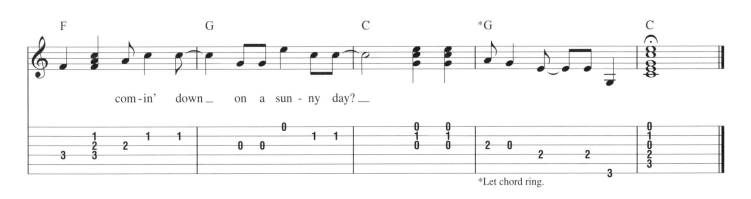

com - in'   down _   on   a   sun - ny   day? _

*Let chord ring.

Additional Lyrics

2. Yesterday and days before, sun is cold and rain is hard.
I know; been that way for all my time.
Till forever on it goes, through the circle fast and slow.
I know; it can't stop, I wonder.

Lodi

Words and Music by John Fogerty

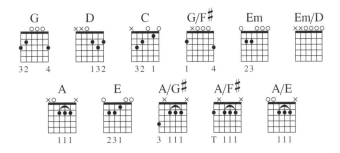

*Capo III

Strum Pattern: 1, 6
Pick Pattern: 4, 5

Intro
Moderately

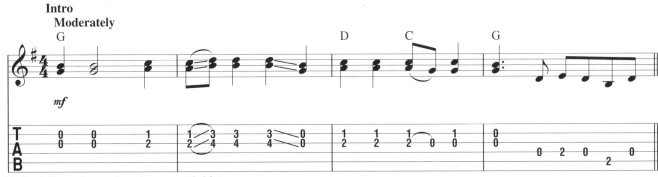

*Optional: To match recording, place capo at 3rd fret.

Verse

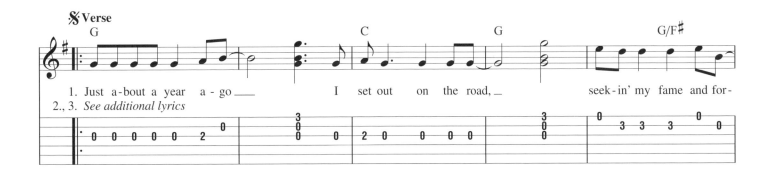

1. Just a-bout a year a-go ___ I set out on the road, ___ seek-in' my fame and for-
2., 3. *See additional lyrics*

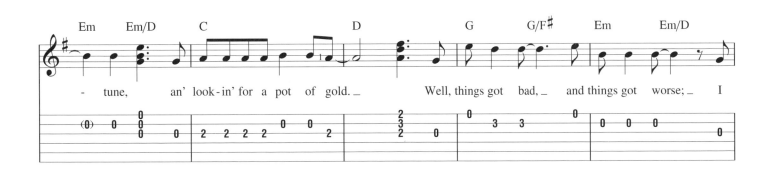

- tune, an' look-in' for a pot of gold. ___ Well, things got bad, ___ and things got worse; ___ I

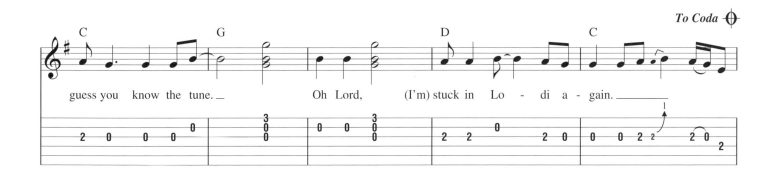

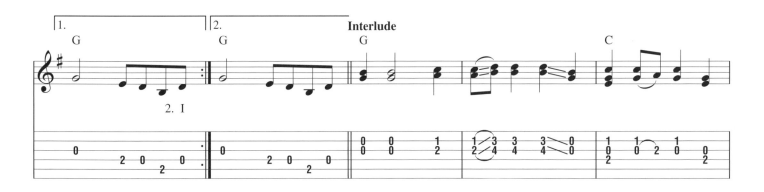

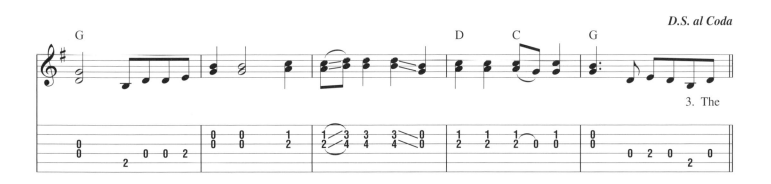

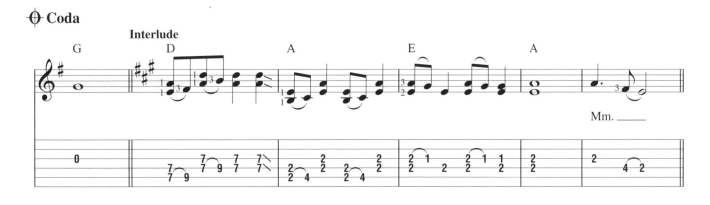

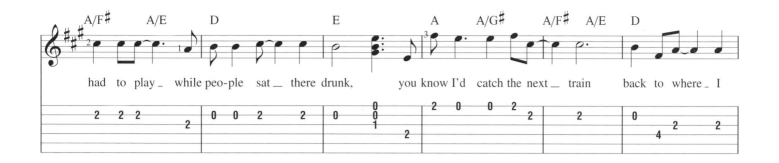

had to play _ while peo-ple sat _ there drunk,   you know I'd catch the next _ train   back to where _ I

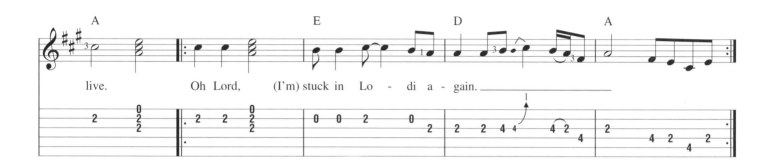

live.   Oh Lord,   (I'm) stuck in Lo - di a - gain. _____

Outro

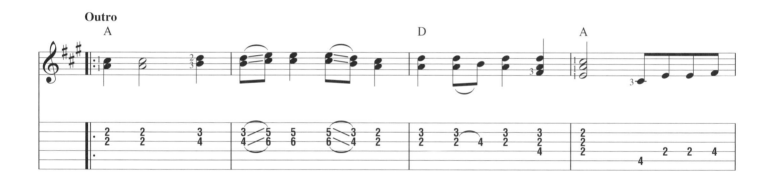

Repeat and fade

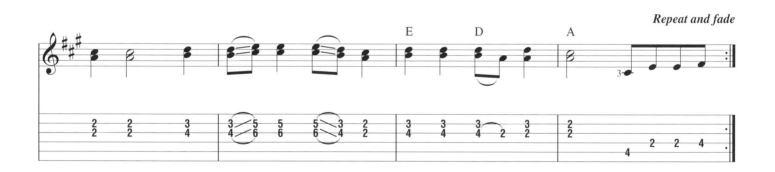

Additional Lyrics

2. I rode in on a Greyhound, well, I'll be walkin' out if I go.
   I was just passin' through, must be seven months or more.
   Ran out of time and money; looks like they took my friends.
   Oh, Lord, I'm stuck in a Lodi again.

3. The man from the magazine said I was on my way.
   Somewhere I lost connections, I ran out of songs to play.
   I came into town a one night stand, looks like my plans fell through.
   Oh, Lord, I'm stuck in a Lodi again.

Proud Mary

Words and Music by John Fogerty

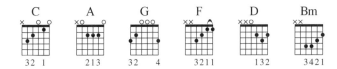

Strum Pattern: 1, 6
Pick Pattern: 4

Intro
Moderately

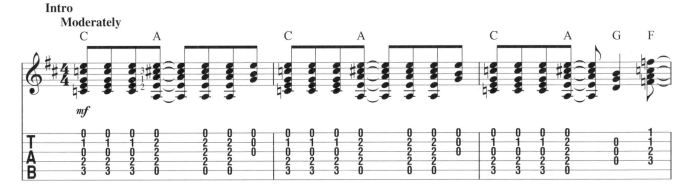

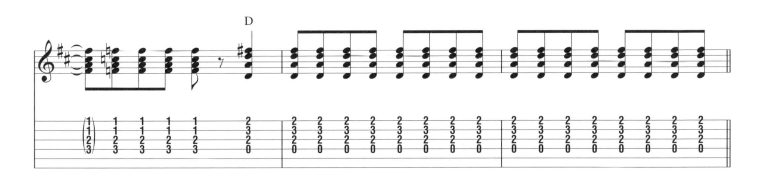

Verse

1. Left a good job __ in the cit - y, work-in' for the man __ ev-'ry night and day. __
2., 3. *See additional lyrics*

And I nev - er lost __ one min - ute of sleep - in', wor-ry-in' 'bout the way __ things

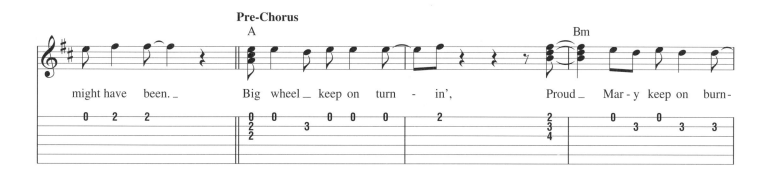

Pre-Chorus

might have been.__ Big wheel __ keep on turn - in', Proud __ Mar - y keep on burn-

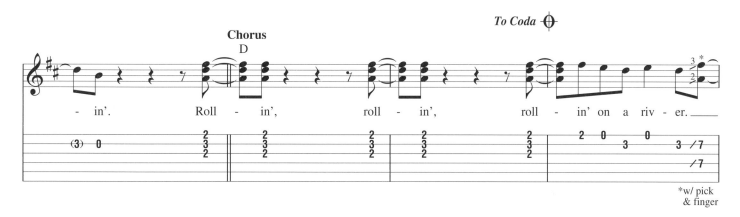

To Coda ⊕

Chorus

- in'. Roll - in', roll - in', roll - in' on a riv - er.____

*w/ pick
& finger

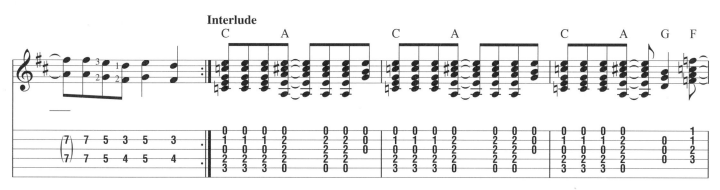

Interlude

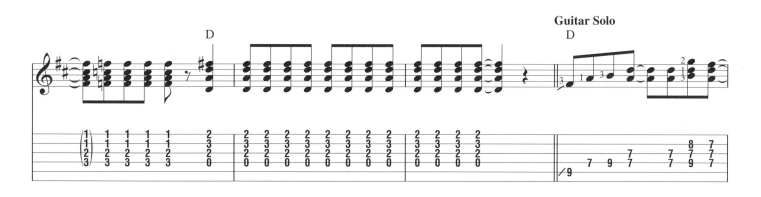

Guitar Solo

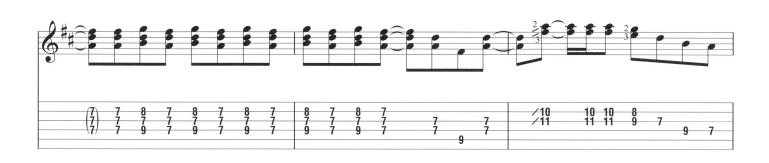

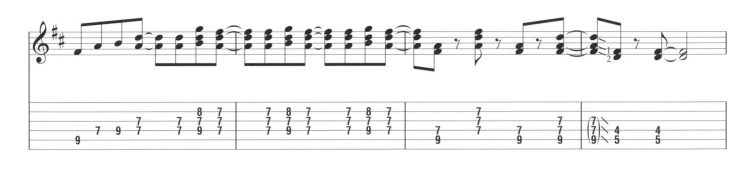

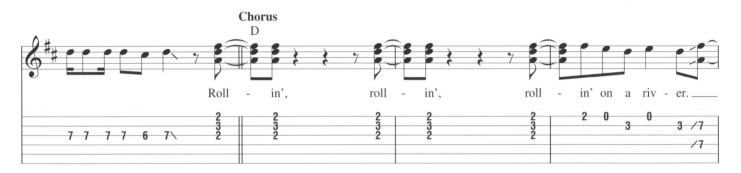

Repeat and fade

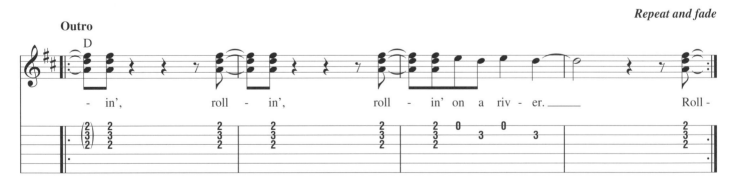

Additional Lyrics

2. Cleaned a lot of plates in Memphis,
   Pumped a lot of pain down in New Orleans,
   But I never saw the good side of the city
   Till I hitched a ride on a riverboat queen.

3. If you come down to the river,
   Bet you're gonna find some people who live.
   You don't have to worry 'cause you have no money,
   People on the river are happy to give.

Up Around the Bend

Words and Music by John Fogerty

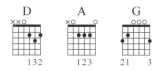

Strum Pattern: 1, 6
Pick Pattern: 2, 5

Intro
Moderately

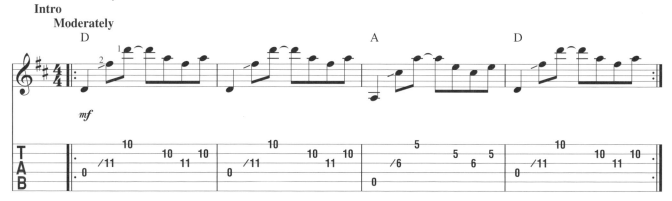

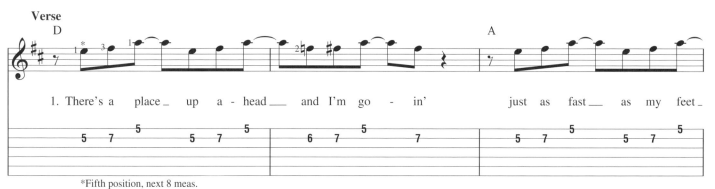

1. There's a place up a-head and I'm go - in' just as fast as my feet

*Fifth position, next 8 meas.

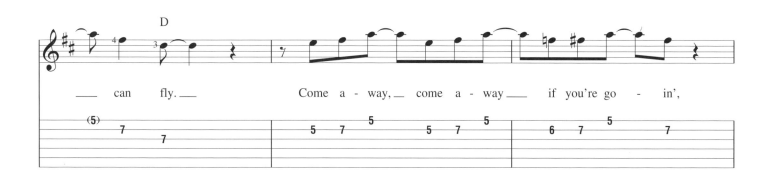

can fly. Come a - way, come a - way if you're go - in',

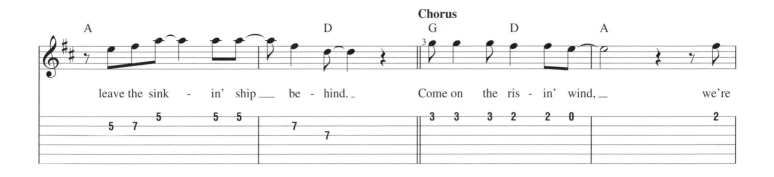

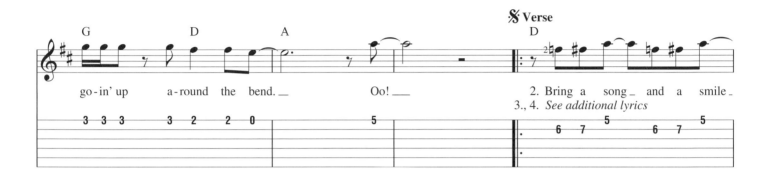

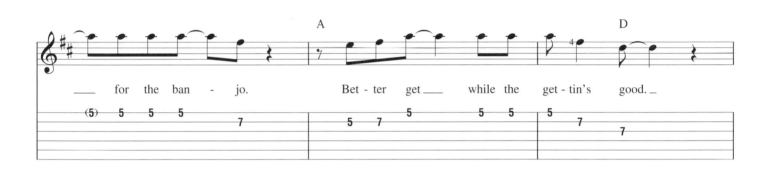

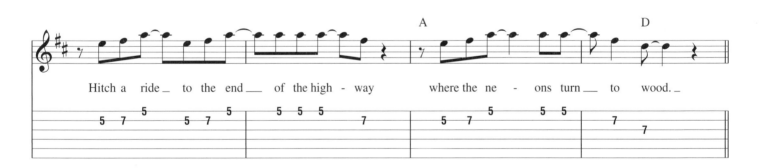

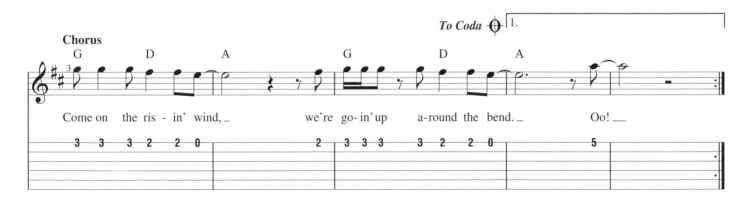

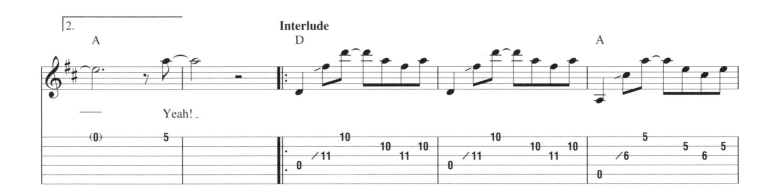

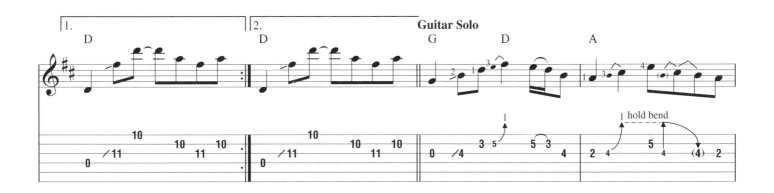

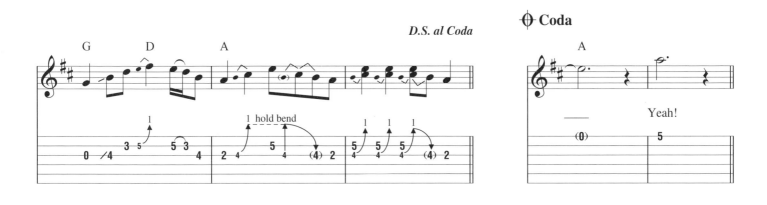

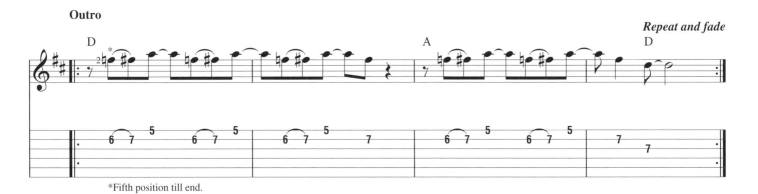

*Fifth position till end.

Additional Lyrics

2. You can ponder perpetual motion,
   Fix your mind on a crystal day.
   Always time for a good conversation,
   There's an ear for what you say.

3. Catch a ride to the end of the highway
   And we'll meet by the big red tree.
   There's a place up ahead and I'm goin';
   Come along, come along with me.

Run Through the Jungle

Words and Music by John Fogerty

Drop D tuning:
(low to high) D-A-D-G-B-E

Strum Pattern: 1, 6
Pick Pattern: 2, 5

Intro
Moderately

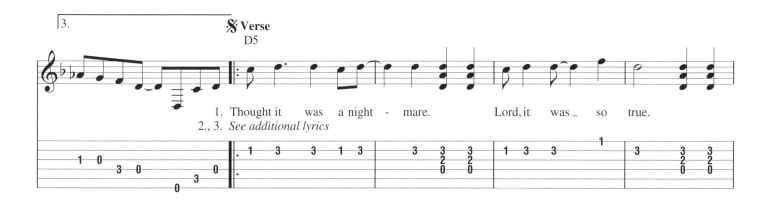

1. Thought it was a night - mare. Lord, it was _ so true.
2., 3. *See additional lyrics*

They told me, "Don't go walk-in' slow, _ the dev-il's on _ the loose." Bet-ter run ____ through the jun - gle.

Bet-ter run ___ through the jun - gle. Bet-ter run ___ through the jun - gle.

3rd time, to Coda ⊕
Harmonica Solo
D5

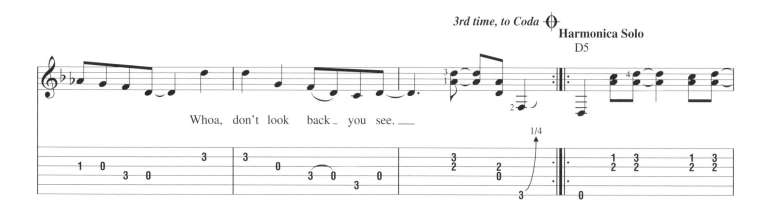

Whoa, don't look back ___ you see. ___

1., 2., 3. | 4. | *D.S. al Coda*

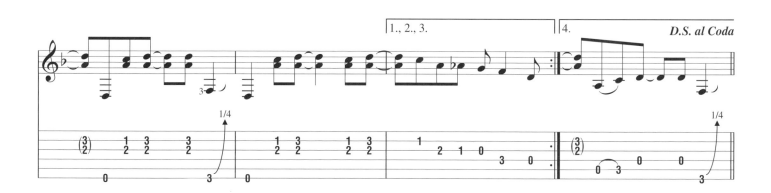

⊕ **Coda**
Outro-Harmonica Solo

Repeat and fade

D5

Additional Lyrics

2. Thought I heard a rumblin'
   Callin' to my name.
   Two hundred million guns are loaded;
   Satan cries, "Take aim!"

3. Over on the mountain,
   Thunder magic spoke;
   "Let the people know my wisdom,
   Fill the land with smoke."

Susie-Q

Words and Music by Dale Hawkins, Stan Lewis and Eleanor Broadwater

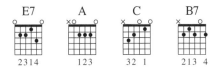

Strum Pattern: 4
Pick Pattern: 1, 4

1., 5. Oh, __ Su - sie - Q. ____ Oh, __ Su - sie - Q. ____
3. *See additional lyrics*

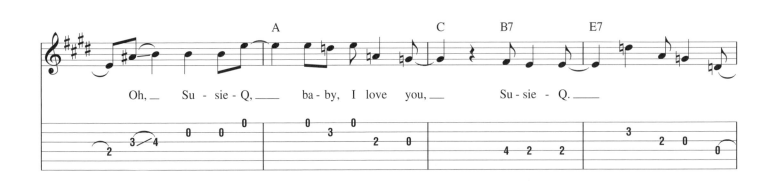

Oh, __ Su - sie - Q, ___ ba - by, I love you, __ Su - sie - Q. ____

2. Like the way you walk. ___
4. *See additional lyrics*

I like the way you talk. ___

To Coda 2 ⊕

I like the way you walk, ___ I like the way you talk, ___ Su - sie - Q. ___

To Coda 1 ⊕

Guitar Solo

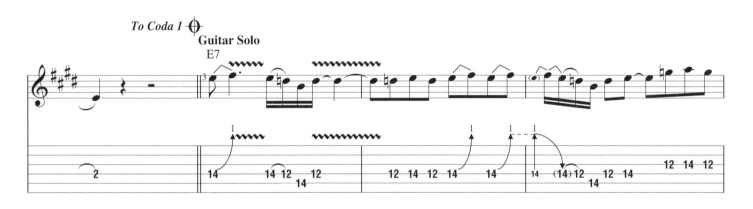

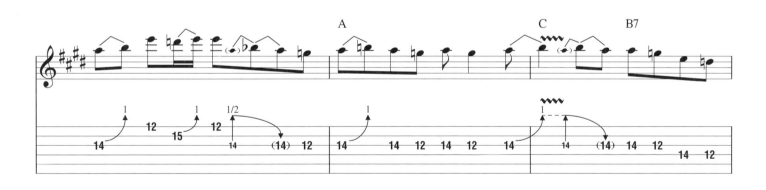

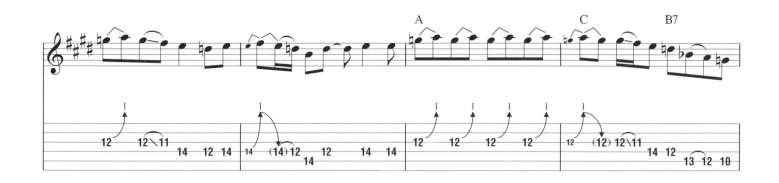

⊕ Coda 1

D.C. al Coda 1

D.C. al Coda 1
(take repeat)

Guitar Solo

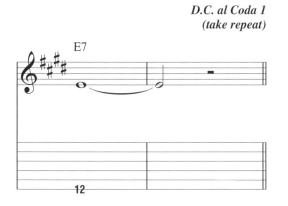

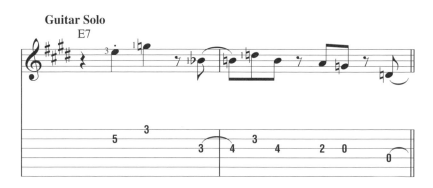

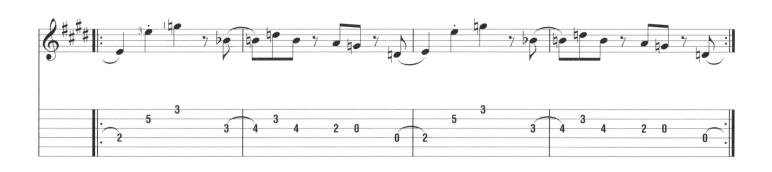

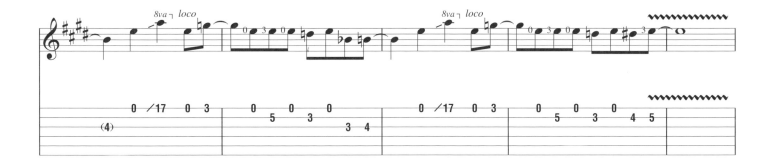

D.C. al Coda 2
(take repeat)

 Coda 2

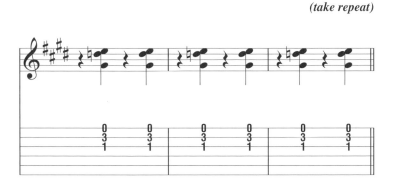

Verse
E7

6. Oh, Su-sie - Q. ____

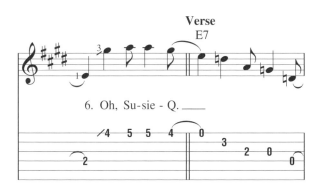

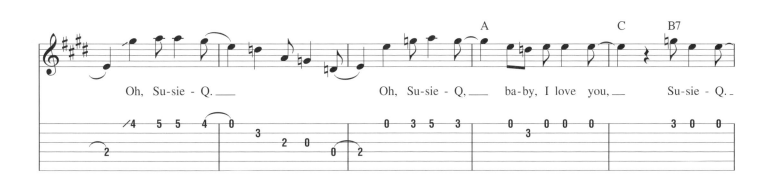

Oh, Su-sie - Q. ____   Oh, Su-sie - Q, ____ ba-by, I love you, ____   Su-sie - Q. __

Outro

Repeat and fade

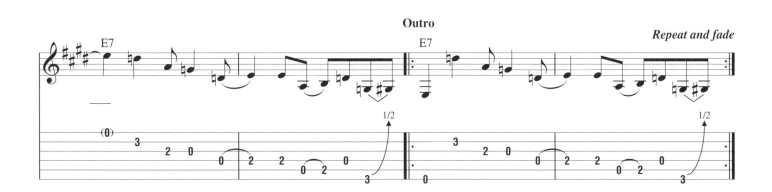

Additional Lyrics

3. Well, say that you'll be true.
   Well, say that you'll be true.
   Well, say that you'll be true
   And never leave me blue, Susie-Q.

4. Well, say that you'll be mine.
   Well, say that you'll be mine.
   Well, say that you'll be mine,
   Baby, all the time, Susie-Q.

Travelin' Band

Words and Music by John Fogerty

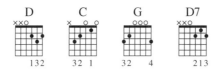

Strum Pattern: 1
Pick Pattern: 5

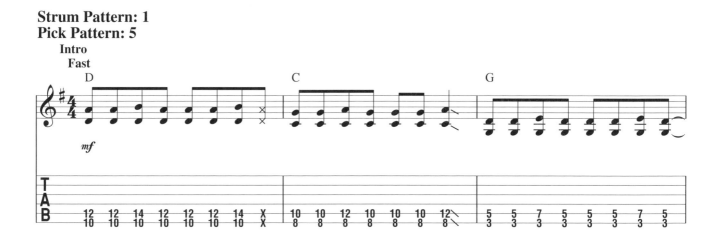

1. Sev - en Thir - ty Sev - en com - in' out of the sky. __ Won't you
2., 3., 4. *See additional lyrics*

*2nd, 3rd & 4th times, let G chord ring.
**Third position

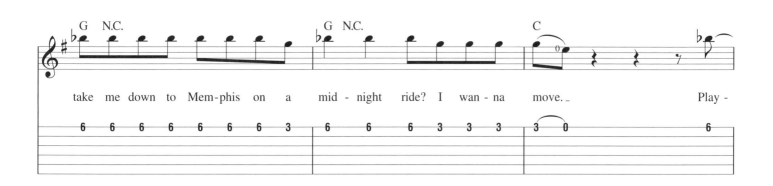

take me down to Mem - phis on a mid - night ride? I wan - na move. __ Play -

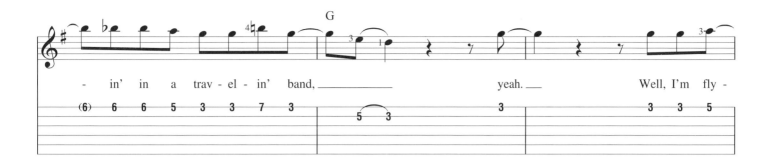

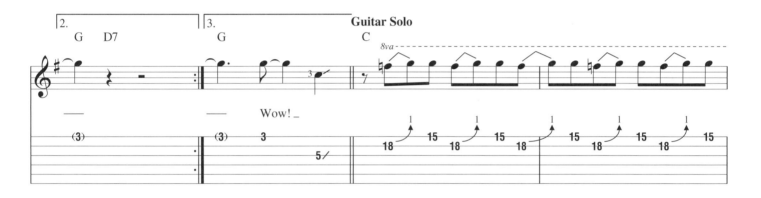

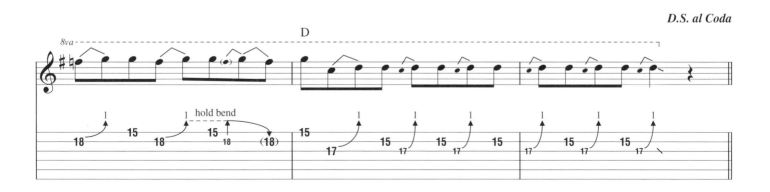

Coda

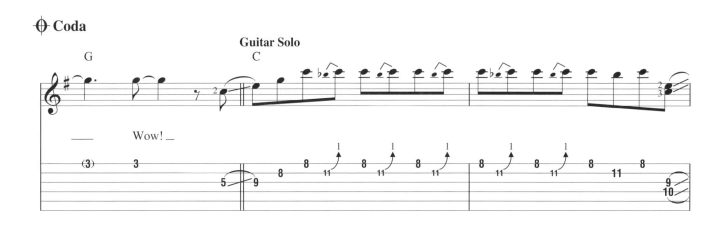

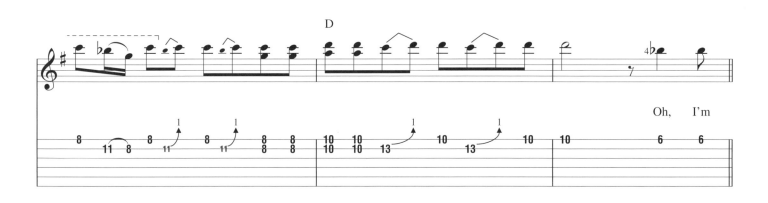

*Barre 1st finger across
E & B strings.

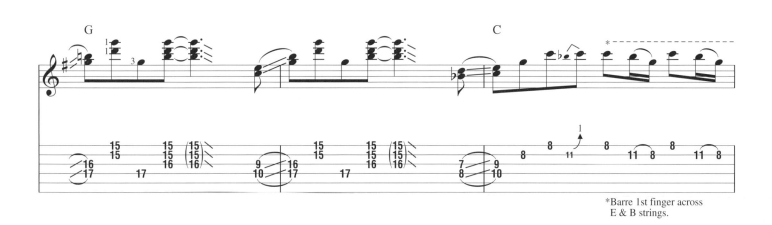

Chorus

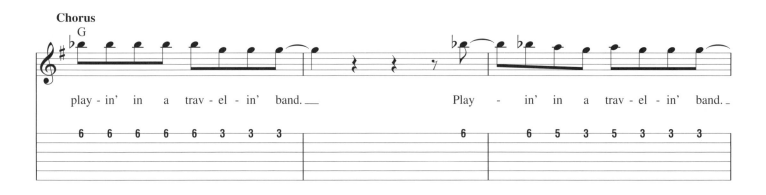

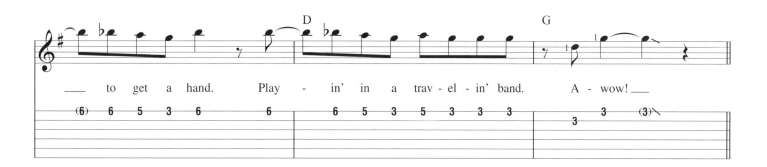

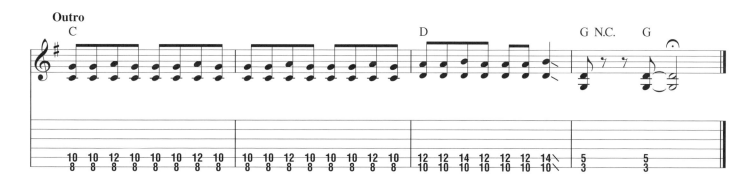

Additional Lyrics

2. Take me to the hotel. Baggage gone, oh well.
   Come on, come on, won't you get me to my room?
   I wanna move.
   Playin' in a travelin' band, yeah.
   Well, I'm flyin' 'cross the land
   Tryin' to get a hand.
   Playin' in a travelin' band.

3. Listen to the radio talkin' 'bout the last show.
   Someone got excited, had to call the state militia.
   Wanna move.
   Playin' in a travelin' band, yeah.
   Well, I'm flyin' 'cross the land
   Tryin' to get a hand.
   Playin' in a travelin' band.

4. Here we come again on a Staturday night.
   With your fussin' and your fightin', won't you get me to the right?
   I wanna move.
   Playin' in a travelin' band, yeah.
   Well, I'm flyin' 'cross the land
   Tryin' to get a hand.
   Playin' in a travelin' band.

Who'll Stop the Rain

Words and Music by John Fogerty

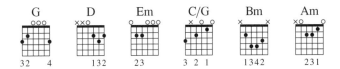

Strum Pattern: 1
Pick Pattern: 4

Intro
Moderately

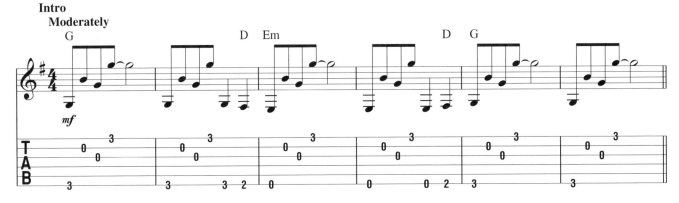

§ Verse

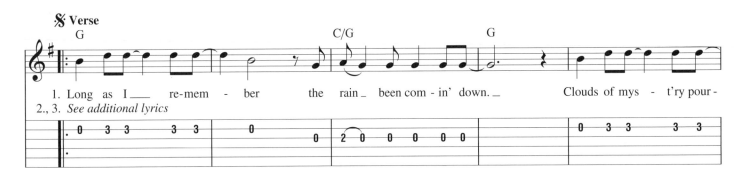

1. Long as I ___ re-mem - ber the rain ___ been com - in' down. ___ Clouds of mys - t'ry pour-
2., 3. *See additional lyrics*

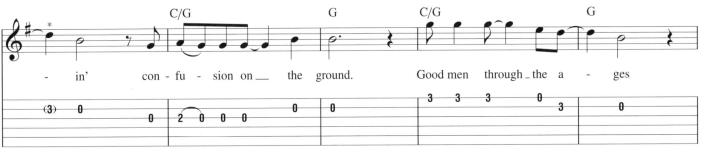

-in' con - fu - sion on ___ the ground. Good men through ___ the a - ges

*2nd & 3rd times, substitute Bm in this measure.

To Coda ⊕

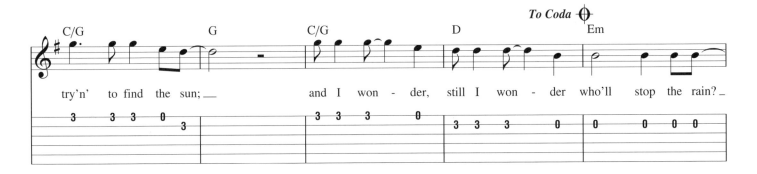

try'n' to find the sun; ___ and I won - der, still I won - der who'll stop the rain? ___

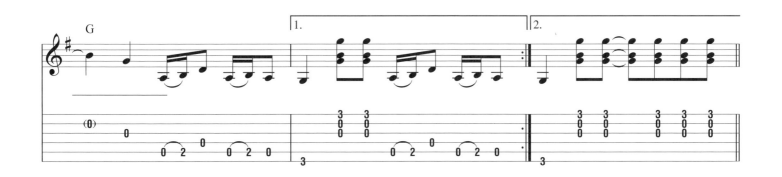

Interlude

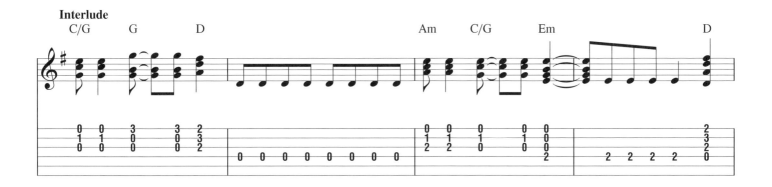

D.S. al Coda

Coda

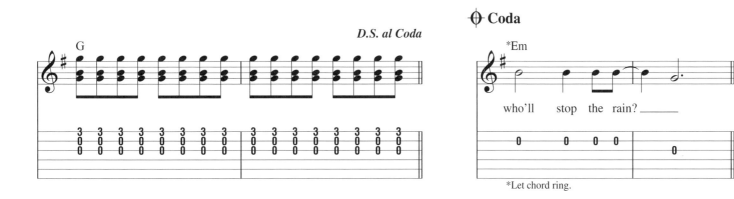

*Let chord ring.

Outro

Repeat and fade

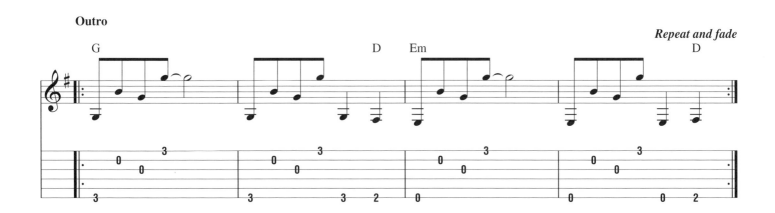

Additional Lyrics

2. I went down Virginia, seekin' shelter from the storm.
   Caught up in the fable, I watched the tower grow.
   Five-year plans and new deals, wrapped in golden chains;
   And I wonder, still I wonder who'll stop the rain?

3. Heard the singers playin', how we cheered for more.
   The crowd had rushed together, tryin' to keep warm.
   Still the rain kept pourin', fallin' on my ears;
   And I wonder, still I wonder who'll stop the rain?

STRUM AND PICK PATTERNS

This chart contains the suggested strum and pick patterns that are referred to by number at the beginning
of each song in this book. The symbols ⊓ and ∨ in the strum patterns refer to down and up strokes, respectively.
The letters in the pick patterns indicate which right-hand fingers plays which strings.

p = thumb
i = index finger
m = middle finger
a = ring finger

For example; Pick Pattern 2
is played: thumb - index - middle - ring

Strum Patterns   Pick Patterns

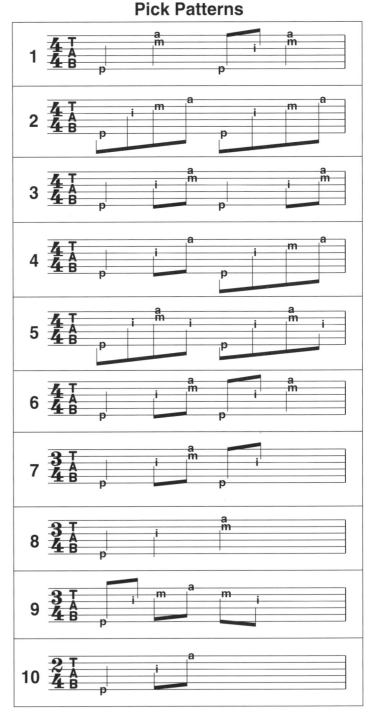

You can use the 3/4 Strum or Pick Patterns in songs written in compound meter (6/8, 9/8, 12/8, etc.).
For example, you can accompany a song in 6/8 by playing the 3/4 pattern twice in each measure.
The 4/4 Strum and Pick Patterns can be used for songs written in cut time (¢) by doubling the note
time values in the patterns. Each pattern would therefore last two measures in cut time.

Guitar Notation Legend

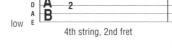

THE MUSICAL STAFF shows pitches and rhythms and is divided by bar lines into measures. Pitches are named after the first seven letters of the alphabet.

TABLATURE graphically represents the guitar fingerboard. Each horizontal line represents a string, and each number represents a fret.

4th string, 2nd fret — 1st & 2nd strings open, played together — open D chord

HALF-STEP BEND: Strike the note and bend up 1/2 step.

WHOLE-STEP BEND: Strike the note and bend up one step.

GRACE NOTE BEND: Strike the note and immediately bend up as indicated.

SLIGHT (MICROTONE) BEND: Strike the note and bend up 1/4 step.

BEND AND RELEASE: Strike the note and bend up as indicated, then release back to the original note. Only the first note is struck.

PRE-BEND: Bend the note as indicated, then strike it.

VIBRATO: The string is vibrated by rapidly bending and releasing the note with the fretting hand.

PALM MUTING: The note is partially muted by the pick hand lightly touching the string(s) just before the bridge.

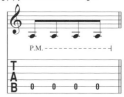

HAMMER-ON: Strike the first (lower) note with one finger, then sound the higher note (on the same string) with another finger by fretting it without picking.

PULL-OFF: Place both fingers on the notes to be sounded. Strike the first note and without picking, pull the finger off to sound the second (lower) note.

LEGATO SLIDE: Strike the first note and then slide the same fret-hand finger up or down to the second note. The second note is not struck.

SHIFT SLIDE: Same as legato slide, except the second note is struck.

TRILL: Very rapidly alternate between the notes indicated by continuously hammering on and pulling off.

TAPPING: Hammer ("tap") the fret indicated with the pick-hand index or middle finger and pull off to the note fretted by the fret hand.

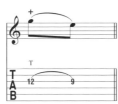

NATURAL HARMONIC: Strike the note while the fret-hand lightly touches the string directly over the fret indicated.

PINCH HARMONIC: The note is fretted normally and a harmonic is produced by adding the edge of the thumb or the tip of the index finger of the pick hand to the normal pick attack.

TREMOLO PICKING: The note is picked as rapidly and continuously as possible.

VIBRATO BAR DIVE AND RETURN: The pitch of the note or chord is dropped a specified number of steps (in rhythm), then returned to the original pitch.

VIBRATO BAR SCOOP: Depress the bar just before striking the note, then quickly release the bar.

VIBRATO BAR DIP: Strike the note and then immediately drop a specified number of steps, then release back to the original pitch.

Additional Musical Definitions

 (accent) • Accentuate note (play it louder).

 (staccato) • Play the note short.

D.S. al Coda • Go back to the sign (𝄋), then play until the measure marked "*To Coda*," then skip to the section labelled "**Coda**."

D.C. al Fine • Go back to the beginning of the song and play until the measure marked "*Fine*" (end).

Fill • Label used to identify a brief melodic figure which is to be inserted into the arrangement.

N.C. • Harmony is implied.

 • Repeat measures between signs.

 • When a repeated section has different endings, play the first ending only the first time and the second ending only the second time.

EASY GUITAR WITH NOTES & TAB

This series features simplified arrangements with notes, tab, chord charts, and strum and pick patterns.

MIXED FOLIOS

00702287	Acoustic	$19.99
00702002	Acoustic Rock Hits for Easy Guitar	$15.99
00702166	All-Time Best Guitar Collection	$19.99
00702232	Best Acoustic Songs for Easy Guitar	$16.99
00119835	Best Children's Songs	$16.99
00703055	The Big Book of Nursery Rhymes & Children's Songs	$16.99
00698978	Big Christmas Collection	$19.99
00702394	Bluegrass Songs for Easy Guitar	$15.99
00289632	Bohemian Rhapsody	$19.99
00703387	Celtic Classics	$14.99
00224808	Chart Hits of 2016-2017	$14.99
00267383	Chart Hits of 2017-2018	$14.99
00334293	Chart Hits of 2019-2020	$16.99
00702149	Children's Christian Songbook	$9.99
00702028	Christmas Classics	$8.99
00101779	Christmas Guitar	$14.99
00702141	Classic Rock	$8.95
00159642	Classical Melodies	$12.99
00253933	Disney/Pixar's Coco	$16.99
00702203	CMT's 100 Greatest Country Songs	$34.99
00702283	The Contemporary Christian Collection	$16.99
00196954	Contemporary Disney	$19.99
00702239	Country Classics for Easy Guitar	$24.99

00702257	Easy Acoustic Guitar Songs	$16.99
00702041	Favorite Hymns for Easy Guitar	$12.99
00222701	Folk Pop Songs	$17.99
00126894	Frozen	$14.99
00333922	Frozen 2	$14.99
00702286	Glee	$16.99
00702160	The Great American Country Songbook	$19.99
00702148	Great American Gospel for Guitar	$14.99
00702050	Great Classical Themes for Easy Guitar	$9.99
00275088	The Greatest Showman	$17.99
00148030	Halloween Guitar Songs	$14.99
00702273	Irish Songs	$12.99
00192503	Jazz Classics for Easy Guitar	$16.99
00702275	Jazz Favorites for Easy Guitar	$17.99
00702274	Jazz Standards for Easy Guitar	$19.99
00702162	Jumbo Easy Guitar Songbook	$24.99
00232285	La La Land	$16.99
00702258	Legends of Rock	$14.99
00702189	MTV's 100 Greatest Pop Songs	$34.99
00702272	1950s Rock	$16.99
00702271	1960s Rock	$16.99
00702270	1970s Rock	$19.99
00702269	1980s Rock	$15.99
00702268	1990s Rock	$19.99
00369043	Rock Songs for Kids	$14.99

00109725	Once	$14.99
00702187	Selections from O Brother Where Art Thou?	$19.99
00702178	100 Songs for Kids	$14.99
00702515	Pirates of the Caribbean	$17.99
00702125	Praise and Worship for Guitar	$14.99
00287930	Songs from *A Star Is Born, The Greatest Showman, La La Land,* and More Movie Musicals	$16.99
00702285	Southern Rock Hits	$12.99
00156420	Star Wars Music	$16.99
00121535	30 Easy Celtic Guitar Solos	$16.99
00702156	3-Chord Rock	$12.99
00244654	Top Hits of 2017	$14.99
00283786	Top Hits of 2018	$14.99
00702294	Top Worship Hits	$17.99
00702255	VH1's 100 Greatest Hard Rock Songs	$34.99
00702175	VH1's 100 Greatest Songs of Rock and Roll	$29.99
00702253	Wicked	$12.99

ARTIST COLLECTIONS

00702267	AC/DC for Easy Guitar	$16.99
00702598	Adele for Easy Guitar	$15.99
00156221	Adele – 25	$16.99
00702040	Best of the Allman Brothers	$16.99
00702865	J.S. Bach for Easy Guitar	$15.99
00702169	Best of The Beach Boys	$15.99
00702292	The Beatles — 1	$22.99
00125796	Best of Chuck Berry	$15.99
00702201	The Essential Black Sabbath	$15.99
00702250	blink-182 — Greatest Hits	$17.99
02501615	Zac Brown Band — The Foundation	$17.99
02501621	Zac Brown Band — You Get What You Give	$16.99
00702043	Best of Johnny Cash	$17.99
00702090	Eric Clapton's Best	$16.99
00702086	Eric Clapton — from the Album Unplugged	$17.99
00702202	The Essential Eric Clapton	$17.99
00702053	Best of Patsy Cline	$15.99
00222697	Very Best of Coldplay – 2nd Edition	$16.99
00702229	The Very Best of Creedence Clearwater Revival	$16.99
00702145	Best of Jim Croce	$16.99
00702278	Crosby, Stills & Nash	$12.99
14042809	Bob Dylan	$15.99
00702276	Fleetwood Mac — Easy Guitar Collection	$17.99
00139462	The Very Best of Grateful Dead	$16.99
00702136	Best of Merle Haggard	$16.99
00702227	Jimi Hendrix — Smash Hits	$19.99
00702288	Best of Hillsong United	$12.99
00702236	Best of Antonio Carlos Jobim	$15.99
00702245	Elton John — Greatest Hits 1970–2002	$19.99

00129855	Jack Johnson	$16.99
00702204	Robert Johnson	$14.99
00702234	Selections from Toby Keith — 35 Biggest Hits	$12.95
00702003	Kiss	$16.99
00702216	Lynyrd Skynyrd	$16.99
00702182	The Essential Bob Marley	$16.99
00146081	Maroon 5	$14.99
00121925	Bruno Mars – Unorthodox Jukebox	$12.99
00702248	Paul McCartney — All the Best	$14.99
00125484	The Best of MercyMe	$12.99
00702209	Steve Miller Band — Young Hearts (Greatest Hits)	$12.95
00124167	Jason Mraz	$15.99
00702096	Best of Nirvana	$16.99
00702211	The Offspring — Greatest Hits	$17.99
00138026	One Direction	$17.99
00702030	Best of Roy Orbison	$17.99
00702144	Best of Ozzy Osbourne	$14.99
00702279	Tom Petty	$17.99
00102911	Pink Floyd	$17.99
00702139	Elvis Country Favorites	$19.99
00702293	The Very Best of Prince	$19.99
00699415	Best of Queen for Guitar	$16.99
00109279	Best of R.E.M.	$14.99
00702208	Red Hot Chili Peppers — Greatest Hits	$16.99
00198960	The Rolling Stones	$17.99
00174793	The Very Best of Santana	$16.99
00702196	Best of Bob Seger	$16.99
00146046	Ed Sheeran	$15.99
00702252	Frank Sinatra — Nothing But the Best	$12.99
00702010	Best of Rod Stewart	$17.99
00702049	Best of George Strait	$17.99

00702259	Taylor Swift for Easy Guitar	$15.99
00359800	Taylor Swift – Easy Guitar Anthology	$24.99
00702260	Taylor Swift — Fearless	$14.99
00139727	Taylor Swift — 1989	$17.99
00115960	Taylor Swift — Red	$16.99
00253667	Taylor Swift — Reputation	$17.99
00702290	Taylor Swift — Speak Now	$16.99
00232849	Chris Tomlin Collection – 2nd Edition	$14.99
00702226	Chris Tomlin — See the Morning	$12.95
00148643	Train	$14.99
00702427	U2 — 18 Singles	$19.99
00702108	Best of Stevie Ray Vaughan	$17.99
00279005	The Who	$14.99
00702123	Best of Hank Williams	$15.99
00194548	Best of John Williams	$14.99
00702228	Neil Young — Greatest Hits	$17.99
00119133	Neil Young — Harvest	$14.99

Prices, contents and availability subject to change without notice.

Visit Hal Leonard online at **halleonard.com**

HAL•LEONARD®

GUITAR PLAY-ALONG

Complete song lists available online.

This series will help you play your favorite songs quickly and easily. Just follow the tab and listen to the audio to the hear how the guitar should sound, and then play along using the separate backing tracks. Audio files also include software to slow down the tempo without changing pitch. The melody and lyrics are included in the book so that you can sing or simply follow along.

INCLUDES TAB

VOL. 1 – ROCK ....00699570 / $17.99
VOL. 2 – ACOUSTIC ....00699569 / $16.99
VOL. 3 – HARD ROCK ....00699573 / $17.99
VOL. 4 – POP/ROCK ....00699571 / $16.99
VOL. 5 – THREE CHORD SONGS ....00300985 / $16.99
VOL. 6 – '90S ROCK ....00298615 / $16.99
VOL. 7 – BLUES ....00699575 / $19.99
VOL. 8 – ROCK ....00699585 / $16.99
VOL. 9 – EASY ACOUSTIC SONGS ....00151708 / $16.99
VOL. 10 – ACOUSTIC ....00699586 / $16.95
VOL. 11 – EARLY ROCK ....00699579 / $15.99
VOL. 12 – ROCK POP ....00291724 / $16.99
VOL. 14 – BLUES ROCK ....00699582 / $16.99
VOL. 15 – R&B ....00699583 / $17.99
VOL. 16 – JAZZ ....00699584 / $16.99
VOL. 17 – COUNTRY ....00699588 / $17.99
VOL. 18 – ACOUSTIC ROCK ....00699577 / $15.95
VOL. 20 – ROCKABILLY ....00699580 / $17.99
VOL. 21 – SANTANA ....00174525 / $17.99
VOL. 22 – CHRISTMAS ....00699600 / $15.99
VOL. 23 – SURF ....00699635 / $17.99
VOL. 24 – ERIC CLAPTON ....00699649 / $19.99
VOL. 25 – THE BEATLES ....00198265 / $19.99
VOL. 26 – ELVIS PRESLEY ....00699643 / $16.99
VOL. 27 – DAVID LEE ROTH ....00699645 / $16.95
VOL. 28 – GREG KOCH ....00699646 / $19.99
VOL. 29 – BOB SEGER ....00699647 / $16.99
VOL. 30 – KISS ....00699644 / $17.99
VOL. 32 – THE OFFSPRING ....00699653 / $14.95
VOL. 33 – ACOUSTIC CLASSICS ....00699656 / $19.99
VOL. 34 – CLASSIC ROCK ....00699658 / $17.99
VOL. 35 – HAIR METAL ....00699660 / $17.99
VOL. 36 – SOUTHERN ROCK ....00699661 / $19.99
VOL. 37 – ACOUSTIC UNPLUGGED ....00699662 / $22.99
VOL. 38 – BLUES ....00699663 / $17.99
VOL. 39 – '80s METAL ....00699664 / $17.99
VOL. 40 – INCUBUS ....00699668 / $17.95
VOL. 41 – ERIC CLAPTON ....00699669 / $17.99
VOL. 42 – COVER BAND HITS ....00211597 / $16.99
VOL. 43 – LYNYRD SKYNYRD ....00699681 / $22.99
VOL. 44 – JAZZ GREATS ....00699689 / $16.99
VOL. 45 – TV THEMES ....00699718 / $14.95
VOL. 46 – MAINSTREAM ROCK ....00699722 / $16.95
VOL. 47 – JIMI HENDRIX SMASH HITS ....00699723 / $19.99
VOL. 48 – AEROSMITH CLASSICS ....00699724 / $17.99
VOL. 49 – STEVIE RAY VAUGHAN ....00699725 / $17.99
VOL. 50 – VAN HALEN: 1978-1984 ....00110269 / $19.99
VOL. 51 – ALTERNATIVE '90s ....00699727 / $14.99
VOL. 52 – FUNK ....00699728 / $15.99
VOL. 53 – DISCO ....00699729 / $14.99
VOL. 54 – HEAVY METAL ....00699730 / $17.99
VOL. 55 – POP METAL ....00699731 / $14.95
VOL. 57 – GUNS 'N' ROSES ....00159922 / $19.99
VOL. 58 – BLINK 182 ....00699772 / $17.99
VOL. 59 – CHET ATKINS ....00702347 / $17.99
VOL. 60 – 3 DOORS DOWN ....00699774 / $14.95
VOL. 62 – CHRISTMAS CAROLS ....00699798 / $12.95
VOL. 63 – CREEDENCE CLEARWATER REVIVAL ....00699802 / $17.99
VOL. 64 – ULTIMATE OZZY OSBOURNE ....00699803 / $19.99
VOL. 66 – THE ROLLING STONES ....00699807 / $19.99
VOL. 67 – BLACK SABBATH ....00699808 / $17.99
VOL. 68 – PINK FLOYD – DARK SIDE OF THE MOON ....00699809 / $17.99
VOL. 71 – CHRISTIAN ROCK ....00699824 / $14.95
VOL. 73 – BLUESY ROCK ....00699829 / $17.99
VOL. 74 – SIMPLE STRUMMING SONGS ....00151706 / $19.99
VOL. 75 – TOM PETTY ....00699882 / $19.99
VOL. 76 – COUNTRY HITS ....00699884 / $16.99
VOL. 77 – BLUEGRASS ....00699910 / $17.99
VOL. 78 – NIRVANA ....00700132 / $17.99
VOL. 79 – NEIL YOUNG ....00700133 / $24.99
VOL. 81 – ROCK ANTHOLOGY ....00700176 / $22.99
VOL. 82 – EASY ROCK SONGS ....00700177 / $17.99
VOL. 84 – STEELY DAN ....00700200 / $19.99
VOL. 85 – THE POLICE ....00700269 / $16.99
VOL. 86 – BOSTON ....00700465 / $19.99
VOL. 87 – ACOUSTIC WOMEN ....00700763 / $14.99
VOL. 88 – GRUNGE ....00700467 / $16.99
VOL. 89 – REGGAE ....00700468 / $15.99
VOL. 90 – CLASSICAL POP ....00700469 / $14.99
VOL. 91 – BLUES INSTRUMENTALS ....00700505 / $19.99
VOL. 92 – EARLY ROCK INSTRUMENTALS ....00700506 / $17.99
VOL. 93 – ROCK INSTRUMENTALS ....00700507 / $17.99
VOL. 94 – SLOW BLUES ....00700508 / $16.99
VOL. 95 – BLUES CLASSICS ....00700509 / $15.99
VOL. 96 – BEST COUNTRY HITS ....00211615 / $16.99
VOL. 97 – CHRISTMAS CLASSICS ....00236542 / $14.99
VOL. 99 – ZZ TOP ....00700762 / $16.99
VOL. 100 – B.B. KING ....00700466 / $16.99
VOL. 101 – SONGS FOR BEGINNERS ....00701917 / $14.99
VOL. 102 – CLASSIC PUNK ....00700769 / $14.99
VOL. 104 – DUANE ALLMAN ....00700846 / $22.99
VOL. 105 – LATIN ....00700939 / $16.99
VOL. 106 – WEEZER ....00700958 / $17.99
VOL. 107 – CREAM ....00701069 / $17.99
VOL. 108 – THE WHO ....00701053 / $17.99
VOL. 109 – STEVE MILLER ....00701054 / $19.99
VOL. 110 – SLIDE GUITAR HITS ....00701055 / $17.99
VOL. 111 – JOHN MELLENCAMP ....00701056 / $14.99
VOL. 112 – QUEEN ....00701052 / $16.99
VOL. 113 – JIM CROCE ....00701058 / $19.99
VOL. 114 – BON JOVI ....00701060 / $17.99
VOL. 115 – JOHNNY CASH ....00701070 / $17.99
VOL. 116 – THE VENTURES ....00701124 / $17.99
VOL. 117 – BRAD PAISLEY ....00701224 / $16.99
VOL. 118 – ERIC JOHNSON ....00701353 / $17.99
VOL. 119 – AC/DC CLASSICS ....00701356 / $19.99
VOL. 120 – PROGRESSIVE ROCK ....00701457 / $14.99
VOL. 121 – U2 ....00701508 / $17.99
VOL. 122 – CROSBY, STILLS & NASH ....00701610 / $16.99
VOL. 123 – LENNON & McCARTNEY ACOUSTIC ....00701614 / $16.99
VOL. 124 – SMOOTH JAZZ ....00200664 / $16.99
VOL. 125 – JEFF BECK ....00701687 / $19.99
VOL. 126 – BOB MARLEY ....00701701 / $17.99
VOL. 127 – 1970s ROCK ....00701739 / $17.99
VOL. 128 – 1960s ROCK ....00701740 / $14.99
VOL. 129 – MEGADETH ....00701741 / $17.99
VOL. 130 – IRON MAIDEN ....00701742 / $17.99
VOL. 131 – 1990s ROCK ....00701743 / $14.99
VOL. 132 – COUNTRY ROCK ....00701757 / $15.99
VOL. 133 – TAYLOR SWIFT ....00701894 / $16.99
VOL. 135 – MINOR BLUES ....00151350 / $17.99
VOL. 136 – GUITAR THEMES ....00701922 / $14.99
VOL. 137 – IRISH TUNES ....00701966 / $15.99
VOL. 138 – BLUEGRASS CLASSICS ....00701967 / $17.99
VOL. 139 – GARY MOORE ....00702370 / $17.99
VOL. 140 – MORE STEVIE RAY VAUGHAN ....00702396 / $19.99
VOL. 141 – ACOUSTIC HITS ....00702401 / $16.99
VOL. 142 – GEORGE HARRISON ....00237697 / $17.99
VOL. 143 – SLASH ....00702425 / $19.99
VOL. 144 – DJANGO REINHARDT ....00702531 / $17.99
VOL. 145 – DEF LEPPARD ....00702532 / $19.99
VOL. 146 – ROBERT JOHNSON ....00702533 / $16.99
VOL. 147 – SIMON & GARFUNKEL ....14041591 / $17.99
VOL. 148 – BOB DYLAN ....14041592 / $17.99
VOL. 149 – AC/DC HITS ....14041593 / $19.99
VOL. 150 – ZAKK WYLDE ....02501717 / $19.99
VOL. 151 – J.S. BACH ....02501730 / $16.99
VOL. 152 – JOE BONAMASSA ....02501751 / $24.99
VOL. 153 – RED HOT CHILI PEPPERS ....00702990 / $22.99
VOL. 155 – ERIC CLAPTON UNPLUGGED ....00703085 / $17.99
VOL. 156 – SLAYER ....00703770 / $19.99
VOL. 157 – FLEETWOOD MAC ....00101382 / $17.99
VOL. 159 – WES MONTGOMERY ....00102593 / $22.99
VOL. 160 – T-BONE WALKER 00102641/ $17.99
VOL. 161 – THE EAGLES ACOUSTIC ....00102659 / $19.99
VOL. 162 – THE EAGLES HITS ....00102667 / $17.99
VOL. 163 – PANTERA ....00103036 / $19.99
VOL. 164 – VAN HALEN: 1986-1995 ....00110270 / $19.99
VOL. 165 – GREEN DAY ....00210343 / $17.99
VOL. 166 – MODERN BLUES ....00700764 / $16.99
VOL. 167 – DREAM THEATER ....00111938 / $24.99
VOL. 168 – KISS ....00113421 / $17.99
VOL. 169 – TAYLOR SWIFT ....00115982 / $16.99
VOL. 170 – THREE DAYS GRACE ....00117337 / $16.99
VOL. 171 – JAMES BROWN ....00117420 / $16.99
VOL. 172 – THE DOOBIE BROTHERS ....00119670 / $17.99
VOL. 173 – TRANS-SIBERIAN ORCHESTRA ....00119907 / $19.99
VOL. 174 – SCORPIONS ....00122119 / $19.99
VOL. 175 – MICHAEL SCHENKER ....00122127 / $17.99
VOL. 176 – BLUES BREAKERS WITH JOHN MAYALL & ERIC CLAPTON ....00122132 / $19.99
VOL. 177 – ALBERT KING ....00123271 / $17.99
VOL. 178 – JASON MRAZ ....00124165 / $17.99
VOL. 179 – RAMONES ....00127073 / $16.99
VOL. 180 – BRUNO MARS ....00129706 / $16.99
VOL. 181 – JACK JOHNSON ....00129854 / $16.99
VOL. 182 – SOUNDGARDEN ....00138161 / $17.99
VOL. 183 – BUDDY GUY ....00138240 / $17.99
VOL. 184 – KENNY WAYNE SHEPHERD ....00138258 / $17.99
VOL. 185 – JOE SATRIANI ....00139457 / $19.99
VOL. 186 – GRATEFUL DEAD ....00139459 / $17.99
VOL. 187 – JOHN DENVER ....00140839 / $19.99
VOL. 188 – MÖTLEY CRÜE ....00141145 / $19.99
VOL. 189 – JOHN MAYER ....00144350 / $19.99
VOL. 190 – DEEP PURPLE ....00146152 / $19.99
VOL. 191 – PINK FLOYD CLASSICS ....00146164 / $17.99
VOL. 192 – JUDAS PRIEST ....00151352 / $19.99
VOL. 193 – STEVE VAI ....00156028 / $19.99
VOL. 194 – PEARL JAM ....00157925 / $17.99
VOL. 195 – METALLICA: 1983-1988 ....00234291 / $22.99
VOL. 196 – METALLICA: 1991-2016 ....00234292 / $19.99

Prices, contents, and availability subject to change without notice.

HAL•LEONARD®
www.halleonard.com

0222
173

THE BOOK
SERIES

FOR EASY GUITAR

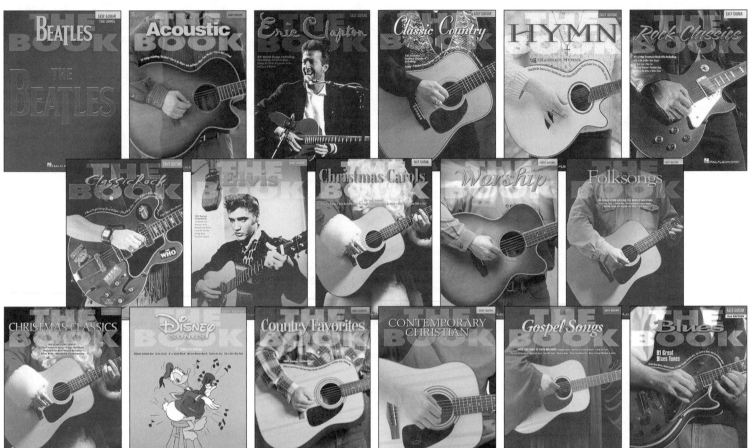

THE ACOUSTIC BOOK
00702251 Easy Guitar $16.99

THE BEATLES BOOK
00699266 Easy Guitar $19.95

THE BLUES BOOK – 2ND ED.
00702104 Easy Guitar $16.95

THE CHRISTMAS CAROLS BOOK
00702186 Easy Guitar $14.95

THE CHRISTMAS CLASSICS BOOK
00702200 Easy Guitar $14.95

THE ERIC CLAPTON BOOK
00702056 Easy Guitar $18.95

THE CLASSIC COUNTRY BOOK
00702018 Easy Guitar $19.99

THE CLASSIC ROCK BOOK
00698977 Easy Guitar $19.95

**THE CONTEMPORARY
CHRISTIAN BOOK**
00702195 Easy Guitar $17.99

**THE COUNTRY CLASSIC
FAVORITES BOOK**
00702238 Easy Guitar $19.99

THE DISNEY SONGS BOOK
00702168 Easy Guitar $19.95

THE FOLKSONGS BOOK
00702180 Easy Guitar $15.99

THE GOSPEL SONGS BOOK
00702157 Easy Guitar $16.99

THE HYMN BOOK
00702142 Easy Guitar $14.99

THE ELVIS BOOK
00702163 Easy Guitar $19.95

THE ROCK CLASSICS BOOK
00702055 Easy Guitar $19.99

THE WORSHIP BOOK
00702247 Easy Guitar $15.99

HAL•LEONARD®
www.halleonard.com